The Scars of the Chisel

An anthology of poetry

–

Compiled in Canada during the
Covid-19 pandemic of 2020

Marius Oelschig

The Scars of the Chisel

Paperback edition published 2020

ISBN 987-0-9948479-7-3

Printed and bound in the United States of America.
Published by Kindle Direct Publishing.
Principle typeface: Constantia, point size 11

Cover design by Dan Huckle, Okotoks, AB, Canada

(danhuckle.com)

Author photo on the back cover courtesy of the Western Wheel, Okotoks, AB

First printing

November 2020

The Cover

On the front cover is a depiction of the "Finger of God", also known as the Mukurob in the Nama language, which was a sandstone rock formation situated 23 km east of the settlement of Asab, in Namibia.

This iconic geographic feature, the result of some 50 000 years of constant erosion, crumbled and fell on 7 December 1988.

Dedication

This anthology is dedicated to my family and friends.

To all of you who served in the armed forces, in whatever capacity, my gratitude and esteem. We, the warriors, are a distinctive breed – only really comfortable in the company of kindred souls. We share the scars.

To those who died in service and those ever willing to make that sacrifice, I salute you.

"Greater love than this hath no one, that anyone their life may lay down for their friends."

John 15:13
Young's Literal Translation

Background

In 2019, two of my friends and esteemed former comrades-in-arms were taken by the ever-present foes; old age and disease. These things happen. In our world, change is constant ... but it can be awfully painful. On this particular occasion, however, I was struck by the passage of time and by the inroads that it was making on the comfortable familiarity of life as I knew it.

I was moved to write a simple poem, which I sent to the bereaved families as a mark of esteem and respect for two fallen patriots and in sympathy with their loss. The title of this anthology is taken from words in the poem, the first in the collection.

I have included a number of poems from a previous anthology, *The Greatest Treasure*, as many will not have read them.

I also decided to provide background notes to some of the poetry. This, I have found, is normally only possible when one does research into poems, and the poets, that one has enjoyed reading. Why not include such information in the anthology? ... I wondered. So, I did. Perhaps this will add to your enjoyment and understanding of the poetry. Allow me a single example as illustration;

The poem, *The Life That I Have*, by Leo Marks, was used by the British for the encryption of secret messages during World War II. The poem took on a far greater meaning, for me, when I learned that it had been written in memory of Leo Marks' fiancé, who was killed in an aircraft accident in Canada, where she had fled to escape the war.

Many of the poems in this anthology need no explanation whatsoever. I hope you enjoy them all.

A good friend, herself a published author, commented that the title, in her view, is somewhat "grisly" for an anthology of poetry. She understood, once I'd explained. Allow me a moment to elucidate.

Our daughter Ana Maria, a doctor, often refers to me in terms of a rickety, old (and beloved, I hope) motor vehicle. My lights (eyesight) are getting dim, the upholstery (my skin) is taking a battering from the sun, the shocks (my legs) are shot, the battery (my heart) needs re-charging, wheel alignment needs checking (one scotch too many), etc. She'll miss me when I'm gone.

Well, like an old car, we all pick up scrapes, scratches and dings along the way. These are what I mean by, and refer to as, the "scars" we all carry. This anthology expounds, in my simple poetry, some of the thoughts I've had - a commentary, if you will – on my passage to becoming a senior citizen, with my own *scars of the chisel of time* – some visible, some not.

Having been a soldier all my life will explain the military slant in much of the work. When reading the term "soldier", please know that I'm often using the word in its generic connotation ... probably more in the sense of "warrior" ... to include sailors, airmen and medics – encompassing the female of the species too, of course.

The anthology has not been compiled in any given order; by theme, subject or chronologically, for example. I trust that the notes will provide sufficient justification for a particular poem's placement.

This is my small gift to my family and friends; the friends I know and those I have yet to meet.

May the wind be ever at your back.

Mooi loop.

Hamba kahle.

The Chisel of Time

Day by day the rocks erode
As the chisel of time chips away,
'Til the hardest rocks on the crust of the earth
Are reduced to dust and clay.

An old warrior falls. A bugle calls
To signal the close of his quest.
With his watch complete, his duty done,
He withdraws to claim his rest.

Comrades remaining to lament his loss
Bear the scars of the chisel of time
As they, who have scaled the summits of life,
Approach the last hill they'll climb.

The chisel of time will chip away
And the clock of the eons will chime.
The rocks will erode, they'll crumble and fall
'Til all that remains ... is time.

31 May 2019

In memory of Keith Fisher and Vos Benade.
Rest in Peace, my friends.

When you have time, like on a long, cold winter's night, take a stab at writing a *villanelle*. It is a strictly structured poem of 19 lines – five tercets and a quatrain – with a somewhat complicated, repetitive rhyming scheme.

There will only ever be one Dylan Thomas. His famous, brilliant *villanelle*, *"Do not go Gentle into that Good Night"*, is the perfect example of this form of poetry, which has been described as "exquisite torture, wrapped into 19 lines."

Forgive, tolerate and try to enjoy my feeble attempt at this *villanelle*, which I wrote while thinking of my true friends, military and otherwise ... wherever they now may be.

A day for toil, an hour for sport,
But for a friend life is too short.

Ralph Waldo Emerson
1803-1882

My Friend

My time on earth is winding to its end,
But it has been magnificent, with you.
I have been blessed to have you as a friend.

As we grew older, so much time we'd spend
Recalling all the good times we'd been through.
My time on earth is winding to its end.

I've tried my best to serve and not offend,
And to be honest in my point of view.
I have been blessed to have you as a friend.

There were certain rules we could not bend,
But if we could, I'd bend them all with you.
My time on earth is winding to its end.

We had our clashes, which we'd always mend,
But our friendship, somehow, always grew.
I have been blessed to have you as a friend.

We do not know how this is going to end
But, God willing, I'll be here for you.
My time on earth is winding to its end.
It's been a blast to have you as a friend.

September 2020

In South Africa, the militants in the African National Congress (ANC) used their own brand of racism, the deliberately implanted hatred of "the white man", to drum up political support for their terrorist cause. One of their most popular "struggle songs", still sung in South Africa today, is *Kill the Boer, Kill the Farmer,* but is somehow not considered to be "hate speech" by the ANC-appointed judiciary.

The ANC has been in power in South Africa for 26 years. Never before has the country been is such poor shape; politically, economically, financially or socially. The people are divided as never before. Yet "the white man" remains the target of hatred and condemnation and is blamed for the country's ever-worsening woes. Farm attacks, often leading to the murder of white farmers and their people, continue – as do the "struggle songs".

Today, in 2020 and despite the Covid-19 pandemic, the Western world is in turmoil as mobs, spurred on by "social justice warriors", gather to protest and to tear down statues of people who they believe are somehow to blame for what they perceive to be oppression and discrimination. Hence my decision to include this poem.

Debate me

Don't hate me, debate me.
I stole your land, you say.
Was it ever yours?
Don't hate me today for what
Your forebears did yesterday;
Trading what was not theirs
For what they could get.
Don't hate me, hate them.

The sins of the father
Fall upon his sons
And his daughters.
You want to be my equal?
So be!
You believe that you're better than me?
Prove it! ... but
Don't pin your father's sins on me.

You said that you'd
Do things better than me.
You've had your chance and ...
You didn't. You couldn't.
You blamed me for the mess
You claimed your people were in.
You've done your best, you say, but now
Your people flee from the mess they're in.

The entire world gave you every chance
And the benefit of the doubt.
You were given all the advice,
And the treasure, that you needed ...
But you blew it.
That's in the past. It's history.
However, it's now time to accept
That we're in this mess, together.

Debate me, don't hate me.

January 2018

To be Equal

I'm led to believe,
By philosophers no less,
That every human life,
One's biblical three-score years
And ten, I guess,
Can be neatly undone,
Detached and divided,
Packaged and wrapped,
And readily stuffed
Into six distinctive drawers –
Compartments, if you like:
Birth and growth;
Emotionality (is that a word?);
Aspiration;
Conflict (of course); and
Mortality.
If that is not equality
In its purest form –
Then nothing is.

June 2015

Write Away! (yes, with an exclamation mark) is the name of a/the writers' group in Okotoks. It is now some ten years old and I've been a member for eight of them.

One day in summer, shortly after our arrival in Canada, while fly fishing on the Highwood River west of Longview, I composed a limerick based upon the group I had recently joined.

The following is in recognition of the friendship and camaraderie I've enjoyed ... a personal tribute to the wonderfully talented authors and poets that so generously welcomed me to Canada.

The Writers' Group

Write Away! as you may have heard
Is a group that fixates on "the word".
So, I scribble and scratch
At products that match
My skill at producing ... a turd.

As we meet for a couple of drinks,
And despite what my family thinks,
We agree, as a group,
That my work is like poop
For, to put it quite plainly ... it stinks.

June 2013

Fledglings

Have you watched as fledglings leave the nest?
Their efforts, under parents' watchful eye,
Is sadly life's first unforgiving test.
Why should it be so difficult to fly?
Yet fly they must, despite the dreadful fear
That ones so young should never have to face.
Encouraged by the ones that hold them dear
They must take flight, ordained by Nature's pace.
Like fragile birds, our children too must fly,
Embarking on their fantasies and dreams.
Too driven yet to see their visions die;
To learn that life is harsher than it seems.
The task is done when fledglings spread their wings.
One can but wait to see what joys our dedication brings.

May 2014

This poem was my entry to a 2019 nation-wide "all ages" poetry contest in Canada. Results were expected by March 2020, but have now also been held up due to the coronavirus pandemic.

Considering the enormous economic, social and emotional damage the virus has caused, there is really no reason to complain about a delay in a literary contest.

Fireflies

Are you enchanted by the passage of a city tram?
Do the shadows of tall buildings bring you peace?
Do you believe that "nature" is a monumental sham
And pray that plans for conservation cease?

Perhaps the roar of traffic is the music of your world;
Perhaps the shriek of sirens makes you sing.
Has city-dwelling always been your most sought-after pearl
And are heaving, seething multitudes your "thing"?

Have you seen the piles of trash that end up in the sea?
And even though you haven't, it's still there.
While "out of sight" is what we do to mask our apathy,
Pollution is the common crime we share.

Have you seen the fireflies in summer's sultry gloom
And listened to the loons beyond the trees?
Have you smelled the jasmine 'neath a captivating moon
With the perfume of the pines upon the breeze?

Can you imagine what we'd do without the butterflies?
Without the bees we hardly ever see?
There's more life "out there" than you could ever realise
Without which we wouldn't even ... be!

Our mercenary, globalising, comfort-driven schemes,
With not a thought for what they really cost,
Will drive our world beyond its means to satisfy our dreams
'Til everything we truly love ... is lost.

Have you seen the fireflies as day fades into night,
Or heard the lonely coyote's haunting cry?
Perhaps the glow of fireflies will help us see the light
And move us all to save our world ... before we let it die.

January 2019

The accursed 2020 novel coronavirus pandemic lockdown in Canada was into its 8th week and morale was low, probably evident in the somewhat sombre tone of this poem.

My inspiration, paradoxically, was a truly beautiful poem, *One Day,* written by another of our so-talented group of authors and poets, Barb Schuler.

Peace

You have experienced it, for we all have.
It started in our infancy, didn't it?
Despite my childish resistance,
I instinctively knew that
I couldn't fight it … and win.
How I flailed and wailed.
How, in my innocence, I despised it.
I wept to avoid it, I begged to delay it.
Then, in preordained submission,
I welcomed it, embraced it … and
Allowed it to gently enfold me. Sleep!
With its sweet, warm glow of peace.

Does one ever forget the lingering
fragrance and warm touch of soft
maternal lips upon a wearied brow?
Or the reassuring weight of a
paternal hand, so gladly received after
a final tuck and a gruff, "Sleep tight"?
And so, to sleep; drifting,

falling on the gentle tides of
anticipation, apprehension,
rampant curiosity and trepidation;
surrendering to a pacific departure
with its sweet, warm glow of peace.

Still, as the years of wonder fled
before my insatiable hedonistic pursuits,
my resentment at the intrusion
upon my quest for novelty persisted.
Until, as the rhythm of my existence revealed
the cycle of impatient agitation and repose,
I came to acknowledge, even to relish,
the circadian draining of my vigour,
the sedation of my senses,
the lethargy of weary limbs;
awaiting, inviting my reward of slumber
with its sweet, warm glow of peace.

'Twas not long before the arrogance, if not
the sheer recklessness of youth,
would see me spurn the gift
more gratifying than any other.
Pushing, punishing the corporeal substance and
the psyche, in reckless pursuit of ...
I knew not what,
with frantic determination to know it all,
to feel it all, to have it all. Until,
in writhing, heaving release of passion
I would again surrender to a familiar embrace,
with its sweet, warm glow of peace.

Long years ensued, crammed to the gunwales
with irksome duty and obligations,
with family and with growing apprehension
for the future of a fragmented fatherland, and
saw me, in desperation, scratch and scramble
and strive to preserve a way of life
which, through pain and passion and
unquestioning dedication, had seen a proud people
live their dreams of achievement and
acceptance. Yearning, I was, unconsciously,
for escape, for conclusion, for respite,
with its sweet, warm glow of peace.

Now, with the maturity and wisdom of
accumulated years, I am conscious of
the wasted hours I should have granted
my body and soul and spirit, to recover
from the hard use and constant abuse,
from the wounds and the scars and the
weariness of a long and lusty life.
I've come to accept, without regret,
that this bashed and bent old body, with its
perpetual pain and encroaching frailties,
deserves its hard-won liberation,
with its sweet, warm glow of peace.

You will experience it too, for we all do.
When does it start? Who knows?
But that instant will arrive when,
for the very first time, we all comprehend
that life is finite ... and too soon must end.

The only solace for us all is that,
despite our innocence, curiosity,
hedonism, arrogance, recklessness
and desperation, there is a limit
to what we may enjoy or need endure.
We will all, one day, receive
the ultimate recompense of existence,
with its sweet, warm glow of peace.

Composed on my 77th birthday, in Canada
7 May 2020

One Day

One day

I will sit by the window, unread book on my lap,

        Gnarled finger marking a forgotten page,

And watch the world pass by.

Words will not rampage through my thoughts,

        Demanding to be set on paper.

One day.

One day

I will sit by the window, finger the blanket thoughtfully placed on my lap

By well-meaning hands,

And watch the world pass by.

My fingers will not itch for fabric and needle,

Thimble and thread.

One day.

One day

I will sit by the window, unmoving, still and quiet,

Breath but a whisper,

And watch the world pass by.

My feet will not twitch to follow the untrodden path,

The road not taken; the deed not done.

One day.

One day, perhaps,

But not today.

Haiku is a form of traditional Japanese poetry. Without going into literary detail, haiku, in essence, is a short poem of three lines with a total of 17 syllables; five in the first, seven in the second and five in the last line. Traditionally, the poem is a complete thought and is in some way linked to nature.

In keeping with the minimalist style, haiku poems are generally untitled. This is thought to have originated from the practice, in the Japanese tradition, of using haiku as a short introductory stanza to a longer, more complex poem.

I was attracted to haiku upon learning that it was used as a valuable tool to teach Samurai warriors patience, concentration, meditation and discipline.

While the principles of haiku may appear simple, and the composition of a haiku poem easy, it is a difficult, but satisfying discipline to master. Try it!

This poem was composed by Basho Matsuo (1644 - 1694), considered to be the greatest haiku poet of all time:

An old silent pond ...
A frog jumps into the pond.
Splash! Silence again.

Think about our world as an old silent pond. Consider the turmoil, the wars, the revolutions, the plagues and the disasters that have occurred over time ....

Splash! Silence again.

These poems, my humble attempt at haiku, are from a previously published anthology, which some of you may have missed.

Laughter of children –
Tiny drops of purest joy;
the essence of life.

Snowflakes gently fall,
leaving a soft, cold blanket
on our molten earth.

All creatures alike
waiting for the light of dawn,
to live another day.

Would there still be wars
on this small, fragile planet
if Nature could choose?

In the soft, blown snow,
the tracks of many creatures –
meandering homewards.

February 2019

Our writers' group, unable to meet in person during the pandemic lockdown, made full use of the internet's e-mail ... to commiserate, encourage, whine, laugh and to share our creative product.

Our "matriarch"[1], Janice Kenyon, got the ball rolling with a beautiful haiku poem ... as part of a short story -

Which I may not use
as it has been entered
in a competition.

This led to further contributions from the gang; inspiring, sobering ... and even hilarious.

I was inspired to write and have submitted the poems on the following page, as a group entitled *Pandemic Poetry*, to a Canadian national poetry contest which, alas, is now also subject to a long delay ... thanks again to the ubiquitous bug.

I am leaving the space below open in the event that, at the last minute, approval is granted for Janice's haiku to be inserted in the anthology. We live in hope ...

And here it is.... Thanks, Janice, for your kind permission to use this poem.

In the hardest plagues
there's an end, finality.
Friends will celebrate.

©Janice Kenyon, 2020

[1] A highly respected elderly woman; the undisputed female leader of a tribe or a group.

Pandemic Poetry

While sheltering in place from the cruel pandemic and the majesty of a rampaging Canadian spring blizzard, these haiku poems swept in on the wind and the snow:

The world our oyster?
Beware! It may hold the means
to destroy our dreams.

The fittest survive!
This dreadful law of nature
brings us to our knees.

An unseen virus
wearing the red crown of pain
now rules our grim world.

Hubris brought us here.
Perhaps the time has now come
For us to repent.

The blizzard sweeps on.
Man and beast cringe in its wake
as the sun peeks through.

Easter, 2020

The Colours of Canada

Canadians view colours differently.
It often takes several years, perhaps even
a lifetime, to appreciate this.
They see colours differently? How?
Well, like ...

Red; passionate, patriotic and plentiful.
White; so beautiful, yet so tiresome ...
... and totally indiscriminate.
Black; the backdrop to a skyful of moon and stars ...
... and it goes so well with red.
Blue; like the water – mostly calm, but clean ...
... and abundant.
Pink; pretty and playful, with plenty of promise.
Yellow; welcoming, charming, but alas, so fleeting.
Green; fifty different shades, with no grey.
Purple; fleeting, unpredictable and powerful.
Orange; cosy, warm and comfortable.
Brown; white in winter and green in summer.

Ah, Canada - where colour is seen differently.

Canada Day, 2020

This is 2020, would you believe it. Left-leaning journalists would have us believe, however, that we're somehow living in pre-revolutionary Russia of 1916.

Yet, the unwashed, indoctrinated mobs are out, wherever one looks, demanding that *their* rights be respected, that *their* conditions be met, that *their* social justice prevail. Wanting more, giving nothing, demanding – not requesting. Ah, the fruits of our glorious institutions of "higher learning", with their accumulating record of declining academic standards and socialist/Marxist political indoctrination in the place of education.

Forgive them, Father, for they know not what they do – and not even those simple yet enormously significant words will ring familiar to them.

However, for those who still remember, some further words of hope to cling to; *This too shall pass.*

You may also consider reading Basho Matsuo's poem on page 15 once more ...

Splash! Silence again.

Change in our Time

I'm weary of disruption,
Of the chaos and the crime.
I hate to see destruction and decay,
But *the times they are a changing,*
And it appears to be *our* time,
'Though I wish *that* time were still an age away.

The only constant in this world,
They're telling us, is change.
It's painted on the streets and on the walls.
And no matter what the logic,
In defence, we may arrange -
The light grows dim for all as darkness falls.

As children we were taught
That nobody could switch,
You were either born a girl or born a boy.
Genders now are fifty-four,
You may change if you are rich,
And the taxpayer will pay if you are poor.

The statues are a-tumbling
And, even as we speak,
New heroes, never heard of, to the fore.
Our way of living is in decline,
Our leaders, far too weak,
And the mob is ever clamouring for more.

I've lived through wars and terror,
Assassinations and the like.
I was alive to see the landing on the moon.
I would hate to see a civil war
And "heads upon a pike",
Although *that* show could open very soon.

The hoards are out, rampaging –
Belligerent and bold,
With signs, incomprehensible and strange.
One unprepossessing poster
Says it all – lo and behold!
Foresightedly, it reads:

"The more it changes, the more it's the same thing"[2]

Jean-Baptiste Alphonse Karr

June 2020

[2] In the January 1849 edition of the French monthly journal Les Guêpes, Karr wrote, "Plus ça change, plus c'est la même chose."

President Harry S. Truman once remarked that, "You can't get rich in politics unless you're a crook". He was not the first, nor will he be the last, to make disparaging remarks about the political class.

"Politics is perhaps the only profession
for which no preparation is required."
Sir Robert Louis Stevenson
1850 - 1894

This Old World

Do we want tragedy? Do we need comedy,
When we've got politicians to watch?
They believe that they're gods, this bizarre bunch of sods -
It's like living with fleas in your crotch.

They bow and they scrape and we all know it's fake,
As they grovel for every vote.
The statements they make, like "No longer eat steak!"
Is like cramming manure down your throat.

The PM we've got, who legalised pot,
An example of someone who's "woke"
Is a political dork, whom I'd stab with a fork
Were I not such a tolerant bloke.

Now, Pelosi and Trump (what a riotous chump)
Are amusing the voters down South.
While Nancy is reeling from all of her kneeling,
"The Don" just can't zip up his mouth.

When it couldn't get worse, there appeared a new curse;
Little Greta, with phobias in tow.
She's the new Joan of Arc, with the true sibyl's art,
Wrapped up in disaster and woe.

Macron hates the Brits and is having the ? 🚚ⓘ🚢?
As the Channel once more is a moat.
While the Brits were around with their powerful Pound
They were keeping the Euro afloat.

That South African crowd, so pompous and proud,
Will steal everything they can get.
They strut and they gloat, on their leaky old boat;
They're the worst bunch of R-soles I've met.

So, let's all shed a tear (or have one more beer)
At the state of our sad old Earth.
Politicians, be sure, with their mink … and manure
Will still milk us for all we are worth.

I've been here for a while and I can't help but smile
At these charlatans plugging their ? 🚚ⓘ🚢
When they're all dead and gone, this old world will go
on
And nothing will change. NOT ONE BIT!

June 2020

Note. For those interested in "breaking the code" concerning two words in this poem, try the Webdings in MS Word 10.

In the late summer of 2020 (yesterday, actually), I drove across the Highwood Pass in the Rockies to Lake Kananaskis in the company of two "fishing buddies", Allan Herchek and Bill Poelman. It is a beautiful, awe-inspiring drive.

Bill, with an encyclopaedic knowledge of geology, explained that those timeless, intimidating peaks had been thrust skyward, across millennia, by the constant, incalculable pressure of colliding continental plates ... at the speed of one-third the rate of growth of a human fingernail. In Bill's words, "The dinosaurs wouldn't even have noticed the change". The mind boggles!

Later that evening, thanks to the smoke from forest fires in British Columbia, there was a truly spectacular sunset over the Rockies.

Twilight Falls

Twilight falls. Sunset
floods the Western sky.
The clouds,
like labour's spume on high,
reflect the shades
of energy; forever fanning,
across history's scriven page,
the flames of progress, spanning
our human crawl
from age to ageless age.

29 August 2020

Yes, gentlemen, I was up at 2:00 am to write this poem.

We're told there's a "boy crisis" in the world. I don't believe it. What is true, however, is that women are competing ever more successfully for available positions in commerce and industry, politics and academia, sports and entertainment, etc., than ever before.

Girls at school are being prepared, and are working diligently, for their ever-developing role in society. Competition between boys and girls has inevitably become fiercer. Consequently, the pressure on boys to perform has increased ... as if they needed it.

Societal pressure on children around the world has changed ... to the very real detriment of the youth. Every parent knows that children can be cruel and unkind. Social media is an additional scourge, which has become a supplementary "tool" in the hands of cruel, unthinking children and adolescents (and adults) - and will continue to wound and damage sensitive children as they grow. This applies to girls and boys equally ... all over the world.

I believe that boys and girls should be schooled separately. Let boys compete against other boys ... and vice versa ... to the eventual benefit of all children.

Above all, I say, allow children to be children for as long as possible. Extend by all means their happy, carefree childhood, for life is hard enough as it is.

O life! thou art a galling load,
Along a rough, a weary road,
To wretches such as I!

Robert Burns
1759 – 1796

Boy Crisis

There is a Boy Crisis in the world!
Boys are quitting school;
boys are more likely
to become addicts;
boys can't hold jobs;
boys are taking their own lives
in vastly increasing numbers.
Boys want to be girls!
This is not me talking,
But the experts ...
Why is it so?
They don't know.

Boys are treated like adorable puppies,
when they're small,
but like toxic creatures
when they've grown.
Nurture your feminine feelings,
They're told ... constantly.
Watch your language!
Mind your manners!
Express your feelings,
but, don't fight, or hunt
or fish ... or drop your hockey gloves.
That's barbaric.

Why can't you be like your sister?
Or Oprah? Or Greta?
Or Caitlin Jenner?
No! Men are no good
as role models!
Just look at your father -
if you have one around.
It's okay to feel inadequate;
that's who you are.
Don't worry. It's normal.
We will always be here,
to take care of you.

We, as boys, were urged outdoors.
We loved it and every boy I knew
dreamed of being a King, or a pirate
or a fireman, or a sports star.
Sure, we butted heads
like young rams or goats or bullocks;
that's normal, for boys.
But deep inside we knew ...
one day, we'd meet a pretty girl,
get married, have a family
and take care of them.
That's what men did.

Today, a boy can't raise his voice,
express an opinion,
but know regret.
He's doomed;
the devil's spawn!
Like that lovable puppy,
he's a pretty pet.
But only for a while -
pathetic pawn.
What would you have boys be?
Be neutered like your dogs?
If you'd only schooled them
to be men, as they grew ...

What to do? How to make good men?
Discipline, from the day they are born
is imperative; like routine.
Give them responsibility;
also, encouragement and respect.
Teach them obedience, but
let them be boys; rough
and tumble boys.
Separate girls and boys at school -
they *are* different, you know.
Then teach the boys the honoured place
Of girls and women in this world ...
        and watch them grow into proud, worthy men.

August 2020

The formal mess night is an old military tradition followed by many, if not all, armed forces around the world. The primary purpose is to foster camaraderie and esprit de corps amongst the members, usually the officers, of a unit, regiment or formation.

A secondary, equally important purpose is to train junior officers in proper table manners, mess etiquette, the social graces expected of a gentleman and in their specific regimental history and tradition. It also gives the Adjutant, or his equivalent, an opportunity to ensure that his officers' mess kit is in proper repair.

Such occasions may also be used to celebrate a regimental birthday, to honour fallen comrades or as a courtesy to a distinguished visitor.

In our family, Christmas Eve is our formal "mess night", when everyone gets to show off their best formal wear; the menfolk their mess kit and medals, the ladies their long dresses and cherished jewellery and the children their new suits or dresses. Despite being a happy and much-loved celebration, proper table manners and formality remain *de rigueur*.

What does any of this have to do with poetry? Well, it has been my custom to formally introduce a new creation at table, at the conclusion of the meal and after the Loyal Toast, on Christmas Eve.

The following poem, which went on to receive national recognition (and some welcome pocket money), was one read for the first time at such a Christmas Eve celebration, in 2017.

Regret

I've stood in the mighty Rockies
With their mantle of winter's white.
I've seen the clouds of migrant geese
In their majestic flight.
I've felt the touch of a baby,
The embrace of a loving wife,
But I've been to war and I've heard the guns
And I've seen men lose their life.

I've heard the lark in the meadow
And the nightjar after dark,
The rumblings of hungry lions
And the jackal's midnight bark.
I've savoured the rain after thirsting,
Sipping heavy dust-laden drops,
As the earth revives when the wetness arrives
And the drought fades into the past.

I've touched the frost on the thistle
When winter sears one's soul,
When nature seems to shudder and shrink
With the coming of the cold.
I've seen the first shy blossoms,
Delicate and bedewed,
Reveal themselves to a wanting world
Rejoicing, with hope renewed.

I've gazed at the works of Masters.
Composers have made me weep -
But, what of the paintings yet to be
And the music still asleep?
So, my only regret at the failing years
Is for beauty that will be denied -
For the many wonders I'll never behold
When the darkness deepens at Eventide.

Christmas Eve, 2017

Zasha, our granddaughter, played the role of Martha Cratchit in Theatre Calgary's production of *A Christmas Carol* in 2015.

That year, when I read it after our Christmas Eve dinner, the following poem flew like an over-fed Christmas turkey.

Bad poetry?

Not Just Once a Year

I don't see ghosts at Christmas, or Santa on his sleigh,
I don't see presents underneath a tree on Christmas Day.
Instead I see a wounded world with conflict everywhere.
Instead of happiness, I see the shadow of despair.

Where has the joy of childhood gone? Where are those care-free days;
The gentle life that children led beneath their parent's gaze?
Perhaps *that* is the reason for this absence of delight;
The absence of good parents to teach their children wrong from right.

Can it be true that there is fruit that withers on the vine,
That rots before maturity, that falls before its time?
Have modern children now become the people that we fear,
Already spoiled and grown and soiled, with no one there to care?

Oh, let the joy of Christmas be found in every home,
Not in the malls where children roam, rejected and alone.
Let every child be cherished, free of want and hurt and fear,
But throughout their precious lives ... and not just once a year.

Christmas 2015

I wouldn't go so far as to say that everyone *should* write poetry, but I certainly believe that everyone *could* write poetry. It's all in the mind.

It was this premise that convinced our local Public Library Board to initiate a programme aimed at encouraging the town's seniors to engage in creative writing ... to involve them more closely with the community. The library duly launched a Senior's Writing Challenge, a summer contest, which included short story, reminiscence and poetry categories.

Participants were encouraged to attend talks, lectures, discussion groups, etc. at the library - free of charge. With a provincial New Horizons for Seniors funding grant, we were able to present this popular event for three years, which included the very successful award ceremonies and small prizes for the winners.

Just before we kicked the programme off, I wrote *Bad Poetry*, submitted it to our local poetry contest as part of the National Poetry Month of April ... and won.

My point, exactly.

Bad Poetry

There are those who will disagree but,
according to me, there is no bad poetry.
There are no bad poets – some are simply
better than others.
Far better, perhaps, or just with greater skill.
We can't all be Babe Ruth,
or Tiger Woods, or Garth Brooks, or
Shakespeare for that matter, but we can,
as best we can, express our thoughts and
feelings; articulate, through poetry,

in the common words we say, the passion and
the pain that drives our everyday.
Like playing baseball with friends, or playing a
round of golf, or singing a favourite song
or losing a job, or being dumped
by the only girl that you ever truly loved,
or spilling hot coffee all over your
new pants at the sight of ...
the new girl in your life who doesn't even
know who you are.
Can that ever be bad?

If a man, who is not a carpenter
is asked to build a bench, perhaps
decides for himself to build a bench; and,
if he should make something
that looks like a bench, feels and smells and
is used like a bench, is it not a bench?
Is he not a carpenter?
It may not be the finest bench
in the village or the town.
You may not like it or want it, but
it is a bench. And if a man,
who is a poet, decides to write
really bad poetry; to scoff, to deride or
to goad. Were he to succeed,
would you agree that he
has written good poetry?
Now, if a man, not a poet, is moved
to write a poem to tell the world
that he has fallen in love, and
someone – having never read poetry –

is moved to tears, remembering that he, or she,
was also once in love.
Can it ever be a bad poem?
Everyone has a story to tell; a unique
wonderful story that only they can tell.
There is no shame in being unschooled,
in fumbling with the tools.
One can always learn. Are we ever too old
to learn?

For it is the story that people wish to hear;
of everyday life, in words
that they know, recognise, comprehend;
that bring them joy, which they can repeat
when their own scabby life
beats them into retreat
from the joy they once knew.
And, if the teller were to choose poetry
as the method of telling, can that be wrong?
Does that make the poetry bad?
What would be sad, would be the failure
to tell the story, to hear the story -
whether or not in elegantly crafted, flowing
magical poetry, prose or rhyming verse -
that will cause even the snotty poetry snob to pause –
to listen to the story.
Then, when the story is written or told,
the poet - good poet, bad poet –
will feel and grasp the same liberating,
addictive, exquisite joy of
Creation ... of poetry.

April 2016

Poetry is simply the poets' expression of life as he or she sees and experiences it. It may be inspired by joy, rage, fear, love, hatred or any of the myriad feelings and emotions that humans experience – like pain.

The words may ferment in the mind for ages, flow spontaneously from an ecstatic heart or tumble out in lubricated exuberance. Inspiration may even occur with a throbbing foot raised on a comfortable pillow.

All one needs is pencil and paper ... and a little imagination.

Focus

I stubbed my toe.
What better way to
concentrate all thought
and focus upon
the essentials in life?
The world may sunder,
dynasties disappear,
and fortunes founder,
but the most pressing
problem to address,
immediately,
is alleviation
of the pain
of a stubbed toe.

July 2020

Last year I saw a programme on BBC TV featuring an interview with a 100-year old English gentleman. When asked about his secret to longevity, he said, “I just keep breathing”. However accurate that may be, it’s a little more complicated than that.

Too many of the elderly fall into the habit of … doing nothing – a slippery slope to social isolation, loneliness and depression. Having led an active, hectic and adventurous professional and sporting life, I now find satisfaction in calmer pursuits. While angling, cycling and hiking remain important, the Canadian winters are more conducive to fly-tying, reading and writing - my other interests.

I have always enjoyed writing poetry, which is both challenging and satisfying … especially as one attempts the composition of new styles and forms of poetry. While the fly-tying caters to the retention of fine motor skills and the creation of practical physical items, for actual use during the summer months, the writing provides for mental stimulation and the intense emotional gratification of creation.

I recently tried my hand (or mind) at writing a pirouette poem. The pirouette, always with a title, is composed of ten lines with 6 syllables in each line. No specific rhyming or metric pattern is demanded. Lines 5 and 6, called "the turn-around or pirouette," contain the same words in the same order, but the punctuation and capitalization may differ. The “pirouette” must be unexpected, taking the poem in a completely different direction. Good mental exercise, while one is still *compos mentis.*

I hope you like my pirouette.

Hard as Stone

I first learned to fight
when I was nine years old.
I wasn't really keen,
but did as I was told.
    My fists were hard as stone.
    My fists were hard as stone.
I guess that's how it goes
when one is a statue,
on a cold, stoney throne;
with granite limbs ... and toes.

September 2020

This poem was born in the Poet's Corner of an Irish pub in the Maritimes in August 2017.

While on a two-week reconnaissance of Nova Scotia, New Brunswick and Prince Edward Island, we were out drinking (of course) with Pat, a teacher, and Craig Jahnke, a rancher – two wonderful Saskatchewanians and quintessential Canadians – when, on a Friday night, the only space available was in the Poet's Corner of said Irish pub.

As the beer flowed, the inevitable happened. Pat and I challenged each other to write a poem. The first verse, below, was my effort. The poem was completed upon our return to Okotoks.

Running from the Reaper

With tireless tread he roves across the land,
A sharpened scythe forever in his hand.
Though watchful eyes peruse his every stride,
We mortals know - we have no place to hide.

For those of us who fear this dreadful jerk,
Who goes about his grim and gruesome work,
There is a way to duck his nasty knife,
To add a few more years to every life.

The first thing you must do is ... have a beer.
It gives you time to think and calms your fear.
Then, using all your guile and crafty wit,
Draw up your plan to dodge the smelly ... twit.

"Keep moving!", is my best advice to you.
"One step ahead!", is really what to do.
Don't ever stop, don't ever quit the game;
He'll get you while you rest your weary frame.

Stand up to him should he approach too near,
Look in his eyes and show you have no fear.
Then scare him off by doing something frightening
Like parachuting, downhill skiing, mountain biking.

He'll get you in the end - you know that's fate.
So, don't sit there like some flabby piece of bait.
Make it tough for him, go out and have some fun
And enjoy those extra years you will have won.

My span is running out upon this coil,
But my lot has not been *only* sweat and toil.
I've burned my candle right down to the nub
So, if the Reaper *really* wants me ...
he can find me in the pub.

September 2017

The word *couplet* is taken from the French word meaning "two pieces of iron riveted or hinged together."

In poetry, a couplet usually consists of two successive lines that rhyme and have the same metre, or rhythm, expressing a complete thought.

Tamil literature is known for the wonderful use of couplets in its ancient poetry. I found one such couplet, translated into English in 1886, to be particularly intriguing ... as it could have been written by an American poet during the "pandemic riots" across that country during June 2020.

Make not thy poverty a plea for ill;
Thine evil deeds will make thee poorer still.

In his tribute to the departed poet Robert Frost, President John. F. Kennedy said,

"When power leads man towards arrogance,
poetry reminds him of his limitations."

Given all of the above, with time on my hands and foul weather keeping me from fly-fishing, leading to a foul mood, aggravated by the moronic behaviour of destructive American mobs and politicians alike, I sat down and wrote a poem consisting entirely of couplets.

Not quite Chaucer's *The Canterbury Tales*, but I felt much better once I'd completed the poem.

Remembering ... in Couplets

Are you afflicted by the curse that keeps one awake at night?
The curse that's called "R*emembering*", a cruel and dreadful blight.
Well, memories are all we have that tie us to our youth;
Like when we roamed our city streets, spotty and uncouth.
Let's not repeat those bitter days, our teenage years so grim,
When all we said and saw and read was some horrendous sin.
Our music, wild and deafening, was judged as poor ... and bad;
Our poetry, they said, was junk; ridiculous and sad.
Our uniform was tattered jeans and Che Guevara T's,
Our wheels were Vespa scooters and the street-drug, LSD.
"Make peace, not war", we chanted at the cops in riot gear
As we partied through the night, smoking pot and drinking beer.
But somehow, we still stumbled on, and made our way through life
Accumulating as we went ... a house, a dog, a wife.
Then slowly-slowly like a slug we shed our irksome trends
And morphed into "The Man", it seems, together with our friends.
We started making policy, we distributed aid

To all the "shithole countries" ... where terrorists are made.
We tried to change the world and to educate the lost,
To bring justice to the destitute ... no matter what the cost.
We unlocked our doors to refugees, together with the scum,
Who brought with them their problems from wherever they had come.
Then, suddenly, to our surprise, the clamouring began
For "justice" and "equality" and freedom ... from "The Man".
We gave in to their plaintive pleas for a just and better life
Which only added fuel to fire and intensified the strife.
For, as we know, a good deed never comes without the pain -
And soon the streets were filled with cops in riot gear ... again.
What went wrong? Who was to blame? And could we have done more
To pacify rampaging mobs and thwart a racial war?
Now, all of this is happening to Generation X,
They're in about their 60's now ... perhaps a little less.
Their kids are the Millennials, that's where the problem lies,
For they've grown up with everything and nothing is denied.
"Sure, go ahead. Piss in the pool", is advice ... but sadly remiss;

For everyone does and we all wonder why we're up to our nipples in piss.
And the first thing everyone does is find somebody else to blame,
Someone else to carry the burden of the guilt, the hurt and the shame.
Dismayed as I am at the state of the world, there's nothing more I can do
Except to pray for the ones I love and hope they muddle through.
If I were asked for some advice to save the world (at last)
I'd whisper two little words that have served us well in the past.
Should I say that Love is the way, for that's what life is about?
Well, when Anger and Hunger walk in, Love is the first to walk out.
Discipline and Respect are the words, the only way out, I confess,
It's hard to admit, even harder to learn, but the secret to solving this mess.
Memories are not all happy and sweet, especially as we grow old;
We keep *those* for the warmth and the light, not for the dark and the cold.
So, while you're sleeping in your bed, warm and snugged in tight,
These are the thoughts and the memories that keep me awake at night.

28 June 2020

One of the curses of ageing is the insomnia. Waking up at 2:00 am, and not being able to fall asleep again, is a burden. Not so much if you happen to be a writer, though. As Saul Bellow, winner of the Pulitzer Prize, the Nobel Prize for Literature and the National Medal of Arts, once said,

"You never have to change anything you got up in the middle of the night to write."

I'm guessing that he was an insomniac too.

The following poem was written in less than an hour ... during one of my "sleep walking" spells. It shows, you say? Okay, maybe, but I went back to bed after that and slept like a log.

Now *you* try doing that.

Thoughts – at 2:00 am

I'm often up before the birds,
A simple thought in mind.
I rise, frustrated sigh unheard,
To wakefulness resigned.

My simple thought soon multiplies
Then, storming through my head,
Like busloads of blue butterflies,
Plans, raging to be fed.

Like fluid flowing uncontrolled,
Like steam without a head,
Imagination, wild and bold
Like Rorschach inkblots spread.

It brings to mind a concerto
Beginning meek and mild,
Then building to the crescendo -
The music loud ... and wild.

A poem forms, then disappears,
The words a jumbled mess.
A poem no one will ever hear –
A blessing, I confess.

A plot emerges for a book,
A character is born;
A dashing diplomat, and crook –
When suddenly ... it's dawn.

Then, thankfully, the sound subsides
As thoughts float from my head
And like the sea's eternal tides ...
I ebb into my bed.

May 2014

The country of my birth, South Africa, is on the very brink of a man-made disaster ... occasioned by rampant greed and sheer political and public service incompetence. The economy is in ruins, the treasury plundered, social cohesion is non-existent and public confidence in the previously robust national institutions (government, free and fair elections, health services, education, financial systems, the judicial and court systems, commerce and industry, public order and security services, etc.) is crumbling.

It could all have been avoided, as the lessons were there, in Africa, for all to see. I've been to many of the failed states in Africa (to hell and back again) and am astounded that the current leadership in South Africa would/could make exactly the same mistakes, only on a much grander, more disastrous scale.

In the poem below, a *terza rima*, I have attempted to condense my thoughts regarding the current situation in and the future for South Africa.

When Shines the Light

I have been to hell and back again
And nothing that I saw could make me stay.
We cannot let the unenlightened reign.

I will ever welcome break of day,
When obscurity and fear give way to light -
Illuminating villains as they prey.

As surely as the day gives way to night,
So will imposters profit from the gloom.
Then, as ever, fearless men must fight.

We need not fear inevitable doom
For darkness is an ever-fleeting phase.
When shines the light, recovery will bloom.

The privations of our cause are not in vain.
I have been to hell and back again.

June 2020

Note. The most common *terza rima*, or "third rhyme", poem is composed of four tercets and a concluding couplet. The final word in the second line of each tercet provides the rhyme for the final word in the first and third lines of the following tercet. The first and the final lines of the poem are often, not necessarily always, identical.

This scheme was first used by Dante in his epic poem *The Divine Comedy*, completed in 1320 – the poem which is said to have led to the European Renaissance of the 15th and 16th Centuries.

Once very popular in Italy, with the over-abundance of rhyming words in the Italian language, the *terza rima* was not equally favoured, for example, by English-speaking poets.

Nota Bene! I would encourage all politicians, of whatever stripe, to read (if they *can*) Dante's poem in its entirety. They will learn there of the "Barrators", the term used by Dante for corrupt, bribery-prone politicians who, in purgatory, where according to his poem they will inevitably all end up, are eternally stuck in boiling pitch for their earthly sins.

I've been watching a story unfold in South Africa; the recent arrest of ANC politicians and "businessmen" for fraud and corruption running into hundreds of millions of SA Rand.

In short, the Free State Provincial government paid some R255 million for the audit and removal/replacement of hazardous asbestos materials from properties in the Province. While the contract was paid for in full, and the project certified as completed, the work was, in fact, never undertaken.

I watched in grim satisfaction as the well-dressed accused were arrested at their palatial homes ... with Rolls Royce and Bentley sedans on the driveway.

This story is of particular significance to me. Firstly, a close friend and life-long mechanical engineer was recently diagnosed with mesothelioma, a respiratory cancer caused by exposure to asbestos. This emerging "asbestos scandal" in South Africa, with its accompanying political corruption, fuelled by greed and thinly disguised as "concern for possible victims and caring for the afflicted" is, therefore, particularly dastardly in my eyes.

Secondly, it was a cousin and member of the political opposition in the Free State Province who first shone the light on this financial scandal. Strength to her arm!

Seething at the sight of those scoundrels taken into custody in their fancy suits, silken ties and with golden cuff-links prominently on display, the old English idiom, "*You can't make a silk purse out of a sow's ear*", automatically came to mind. My Afrikaans-speaking friends will want to remind me of their own, very descriptive, saying, "Bo bont, onder stront".[3]

---

[3] To put it delicately, "Flashy outside, excrement inside".

Exposure

The African custom of saying things
is music to the ears
of anyone who hates display,
like flashy cars and diamond rings,
... which modern politicians flaunt
to show they've "made the grade",
when all they're really showing
is their corruption on parade.

"It's only *crooked* politicians
who ever make it rich",
a US President once said,
as he scratched an angry itch.
"Publicity is a cruel bitch" –
another saying from the Yanks;
something all Fat Cats should heed
while trotting (chuckling) to their banks.

The English coined a useful phrase
in Fourteen-Ninety-Six;
a phrase that, to this very day,
to politicians sticks.
One cannot make a silken purse,
that phrase is said to go,
from muddy little piggies' ears ...
as all piggy-farmers know.

In Africa, the common folk
live closer to the land;
they listen to the drums at night;
they read tidings in the sand.
They're familiar with all creatures
that are living on this earth;
they know what's right and what is real
and what a man's word is worth.

So, let me share a saying,
Out of Africa, truth be told -
that stems from centuries ago,
as they watched the world unfold;
The higher up a monkey climbs
into a forest tree,
the more his ugly backside
is exposed ... for all to see.

3 October 2020

... and wasn't it Barack Obama, of all people, who told a crowd at a campaign event in 2008 that, "You can put lipstick on a pig, but it's still a pig"?

I Choose Dawn

Were I to choose, my choice would be for dawn -
Though twilight, and its promise of repose
Is much revered and thus preferred by those
Whom to a gentler, measured life are drawn.
While rest remains a vital, soothing balm,
Crucial for we feeble beings to thrive,
How does one tame the fervour and the drive
Of those who loathe the ennui of calm?
For them who cannot wait for day to break
The banishing of darkness is a gift,
Imparting motivation to persist
In seeking out the nobler path to take.
I must choose dawn; its energising light
Dispels the languid remnants of the night.

May 2020

"Ex Africa semper aliguid novi".
(Always something new out of Africa)
Pliny the Elder (ad 23-79)

One can take an African out of the bush, but not the bush out of an African. This is particularly true of the many thousands of South Africans, of all races, who find themselves on "foreign" soil, far from "home" and pining for the "bush".

The deep tragedy of this statement will only be fully understood by future historians as they analyse, with hindsight, the tragic consequences of driving so many of the country's best sons and daughters from their beloved homeland ... for purely political purposes – by greedy, self-interested politicians.

I have a good friend in the UK, a former Rhodesian soldier, Colonel Jerry Strong, who also pines for Africa. We take pleasure in forwarding e-mail, WhatsApp and other electronic images of African wildlife to each other ... for the pure enjoyment of seeing once more the land and the creatures that we yet so love.

While Africa may always deliver something new, it yields some of the oldest rites and truths of nature, still evident and relevant in our modern world. While change may well be constant, the natural instincts and behaviour of centuries-old ancestors may be seen and experienced in the natural world to this very day ... exemplified by the habits, rituals and behaviour of the formidable and stately African elephants.

The Birthing Dance

When each new African elephant is born
The joy it brings is splendid to behold.
The herd will often celebrate 'til dawn
As they welcome the new calf into the fold.
With stomping feet and swaying trunks held high
The happiness migrates beyond the herd.
With clouds of dust that spiral to the sky
All other creatures know what has occurred.
As predators arrive and seek to prey
They're discouraged by the obstacles they face.
Confronted by a sturdy wall of grey,
They can only turn and slink off in disgrace.
The Birthing Dance when each new calf arrives
Should teach us all why elephants survive.

March 2020

Note. This poem began when I was a lieutenant serving with 1 Parachute Battalion in the Eastern-Caprivi, in 1966.

I remembered some fragments, kicked them around and fit them for purpose, as soldiers do – some 54 years later.

Just can't expel the bush, it seems.

This is in remembrance of Pongo, a lovable, faithful Maltese Poodle with the heart of a lion. He was the canine embodiment of the expression, “size doesn’t matter” ... a fighter and a friend, to the very end.

Our kids have just acquired a Biewer Terrier puppy. He’s tiny and is the friendliest little guy, but he too thinks he is a Bull Mastiff.

If you’re a “dog person”, perhaps you’ll recognise your own particular friend in this little rhyme.

Your Dog

Who will lift you up when you are down?
A dog.
Who doesn’t care if you are King or Clown?
A dog.
Who will love you when you’re drunk,
When you’ve acted like a skunk,
And to the very bottom sunk?
Your dog.

Who doesn’t care if you are rich or broke?
A dog.
Doesn’t care if you’re a chick or a bloke?
A dog.
Who’ll be quiet when he’s told?
Who will warm you when you’re cold?
Who will love you when you’re old?
Your dog.

Who can carry off a name like Fudge or Spike?
A dog.
Who will eat the scraps of food that you don't like?
A dog.
Who cheered you up when you were low?
Who was around to watch you grow ...
But is now also getting slow?
Your dog.

There is no way you can repay your friend
Except by being there for him, at the end.
He will look you in the eye
As you prepare to watch him die ...
And he'll kiss you when you cry;
Your dog.

August 2020

This poem is based upon an actual incident involving our kids' terrier puppy, Zulu. He's an adorable whirlwind; friends with everyone ... but requires constant attention. With children at work and grandchildren at school, we are his go-to "doggy day-care".

Out on the acreage, his "home turf", for his early-morning "constitutional", he was spotted and stalked by a prairie fox before being rescued, unscathed, by our daughter. The poem tells the rest of the morning's story.

After lunch, with Zulu asleep in his basket, I was reading Robert Browning's poetry. His *Meeting at Night* is a poem with the unusual ABCCBA rhyming scheme. I took up the challenge and wrote about the events of the morning.

Purely Rhetorical

I was in the garden with the dog today,
With autumn leaves upon the ground.
A small black-spotted terrier, he
Was unaware of the owl in a tree.
Before that owl came swooping down
I grabbed the pup and strode away.

Now, was I kind to the little whelp
Or cruel to the starving owl?
The ethics are a mystery;
Where should lie my loyalty?
With an assassin, low and foul
Or with a pup in peril, needing help?

September 2020

As Robert Browning's beautiful poem, *Meeting at Night*, is in the public domain, it is truly a great pleasure to share it here with you ... even though his celebrated composition makes my effort look like one of Zulu's little turds on the lawn.

Meeting at Night

The gray sea and the long black land;
And the yellow half-moon large and low
And the startled little waves that leap
In fiery ringlets from their sleep,
As I gain the cove with pushing prow,
And quench its speed i' the slushy sand.

Then a mile of warm sea-scented beach;
Three fields to cross till a farm appears;
A tap at the pane, the quick sharp scratch
And blue spurt of a lighted match,
And a voice less loud, through joys and fears,
Than the two hearts beating each to each!

Robert Browning
1812 - 1899

June in Alberta, Canada is magnificent. One is able to sleep through the night with open windows ... and the sun rises at around 5:30 am. What a change from winter!

The only drawback is the constant, raucous singing of the American Robins just before dawn. Should one be fortunate enough to have a home within the territory of a cocky alpha Robin, be prepared for your wake-up call at around 4:15 am ... as has been our early summertime experience here in Canada. Tore Slagsvold of Oslo University made a fascinating study into this phenomenon.[4]

Our normal practice, after the morning song of the resident Robin, was to rise, have a cup of coffee and watch the news on TV before starting the day in earnest. What with the (June 2020) constant barrage of bad news from the USA – riots, looting, hand-wringing and political pontification – it became tedious and demoralising ... so we stopped watching the news.

Who needs the constant drip, drip, drip of depressing new coronavirus statistics and the shocking images of mindless youth on the loose in major cities of the world, destroying property, burning and looting? Instead of celebrating Spring, with its promise of new beginnings, we were disheartened by the cruel new reality of a devastating virus and mindless, rampaging mobs. My dark mood spawned this somewhat sombre sonnet.

---

[4] "Dawn and dusk singing of male American Robins in relation to female behaviour", 1996

A Song of Peace?

Have you heard the robin's morning song?
Melodic though it sounds to those who hear,
Its purpose, not romantic, has been warlike all along;
It's meant to render caution, anxiety and fear.
Like the war-dance of the warriors of yore,
With their drumming and chanting through the night,
The intent was not artistic, as they prepared for war,
But to terrify the foe and spawn courage for the fight.
And the "social justice" chants we hear them sing,
Which seem so level-headed to the sympathetic ear?
We should heed the prudent lesson that Nature seeks to bring;
To reject the Siren's song and not surrender to our fear.
What ensues from the melodies that those pretty robins make?
A trail of dead and dying robins in the hostile victor's wake.

June 2020

"Hence, it may be particularly important for male robins to sing at dawn ... to repel potential cuckolders".

Tore Slagsvold, February 1996

My Grandson's Lockdown Lament

The lockdown came at such a bad time;
In the tenth of my grade-school years.
At that stage of my life I was doing just fine,
Getting shot of my childhood fears.

My T&T[5] skills were better than fair –
I'd competed in Texas ... and won.
My six-pack was awesome, and so was my hair,
And my friendship with girls had begun.

October is coming – but coming so slow –
When I'll be a man ... at last.
I'll be sixteen years old and raring to go
With my first-ever wheels – what a blast!

Then the Wuhanflu came and ruined my play;
My social intents shot to hell.
No movies, no girls, no dancing, no way
To survive in my tight lockdown shell.

Living out in the sticks, at the top of a hill
With nary a human in sight.
We're still in the grip of the wintery chill
When the days are as bleak as the night.

[5] Trampoline & Tumbling

Day-to-day life is like living alone.
Then things turned impossibly worse.
They've decided we'll do all our schooling at home
Which, trust me on this, is a curse.

Books are my buddies, the e-mail my chum.
And the internet? Bane of my life!
I do projects and tasks, with tons more to come;
It's worse than having a wife.

My body is flabby; not that of a champ,
And will take several months to restore.
I fear that the skill I've acquired on the tramp'
Will ne'er be the same as before.

Oh, hurry October – my Scorpio sign –
Make all of my woes disappear.
With a license to drive and that pearled-oyster mine
... I'm expecting a far better year.

May 2020

... and so the scarring begins, Zed.

Four more pirouettes, just for fun. Remember? Ten lines of six syllables each, with an about-face in the middle.

A Cold Day in Hell

The Tartar on the steppes,
the Rebel, with his yell,
had nought in common but,
When they wouldn't fight, 'twas
    the first cold day in Hell.
    The first cold day in Hell
Was when a lawyer came.
He'd never lost a case
and only truth would tell;
he sought fairness, not fame.

The Songbird

A bird I'd like to be,
but only in the Spring.
I cannot be a bird;
I do not have a wing -
    if only I could sing.
    If only I could sing
and tell the cops the truth
I wouldn't be at risk,
my life upon a string.
Please, let me see a sleuth.

A Better Way

We should all live our lives
in both hard work and play.
It will be very harsh!
I am here to stay, so ...
    let me show you the way.
    Let me show you the way
To plant a citrus tree.
Don't plant it in the clay.
It's the same for any tree,
but "citrus" sounds so gay.

Lost

I was completely lost
and stopped to ask the way.
I went into a store
and thought, to my dismay -
    I have been here before.
    I have been here before,
I still remember when;
they took my tonsils out
when I was only ten –
and now I'm back for more.

September 2020

Growing up, our grandchildren loved Dr Seuss and his memorable, melodic rhymes. Who can ever forget his "One fish, two fish, red fish, blue fish"? ... and so much more.

I too wrote silly rhymes for my grandchildren when they were sprogs. Perhaps they'll read them to their own children one day.

How better to convey the important lessons of a good work ethic, discipline, responsibility, frugality, historical precedent and the inevitable consequences of easy living and debauchery than via simple doggerel ... or nursery rhymes?

The following is not quite a nursery rhyme, but is meant to provide some commentary on the social issues of the day - as nursery rhymes once did.

All Roads Lead to Rome ...

... if you're not careful

Feral cats will multiply
If fed and watered well.
Cats enjoy benevolence ...
And the Roman Empire fell.

Fat and lazy is a threat
Not only to the cats.
But no one cares for history
While they're getting fat.

Social justice has a place
When things are going well.
But someone has to do the work ...
And the Roman Empire fell.

It's great to spread the wealth
When it's someone else's cash.
What happens when the dough is done?
No cake for your birthday bash!

What to do when suddenly
There's no water in the well?
Try to find an engineer ...
And the Roman Empire fell.

Survival of the fittest
Is Nature's brutal law.
It happens to humanity
Where the capable endure.

Nero was a Roman
Who played the fiddle well.
He loved his Roman orgies ...
And the Roman Empire fell.

November 2013

Mountains and Trees

From the window of my study I see
the perpetual motion of leaves
from a dense stand of Cottonwoods
and, on the distant horizon, like
some narcissistic, reclining temptress,
the brooding splendour of the Rockies.

The mountains and the trees;
constant reminders of the persistent
passage of time – each season lavishly
flaunting its unique contribution
of beauty, pleasure ... and hurt -
attired in the appropriate regalia.

Oblivious to and unmoved by
the momentous events in *my* life,
the Cottonwoods and the Rockies
serenely weather whatever *they*
are compelled to face; mystifyingly
dispensing solace in my turmoil.

August 2020

While stationed in France as the Defence Attaché to our Embassy in Paris, I was privileged to visit many of the military cemeteries for those who perished in Europe during the First and Second World Wars.

As a soldier, and a South African, it was gratifying to see how meticulously the cemeteries and war graves all over France, and especially at Delville Wood, were kept and maintained.

For those who do not know, the Delville Wood South African National Memorial is a World War I memorial located near the commune of Longueval in the Somme Department of France. It is opposite the Delville Wood Commonwealth War Graves Commission Cemetery and, as a small piece of South Africa in France, was in my "bailiwick" as the military representative at the Embassy.

What touched me, deeply, was the large number of headstones in many of the cemeteries bearing, instead of a name, the simple inscription, "Known but to God".

While still in Paris, I made some notes, but never got around to completing the poem I was moved to write. It was only many years later, when my life calmed down sufficiently, here in Canada, that I managed to do so.

Known but to God

There was a light in his eyes as the soldier died,
A light that nobody would see.
'Twas a glint of pride in the knowledge he'd died
For his calling — defending the free.

Despite what he saw of the horrors of War,
He was ready to do what was right.
So, together he stood, with others who would;
Warriors, willing to fight.

With his terrible skill to maim and to kill,
There were few who respected his role.
Yet, without any thought for the freedom he brought,
There were many who damned his soul.

Though he spent all his time in the dirt and the grime,
With the Angel of Death above,
There was always a part of his hardened heart
That yearned for peace and love.

He was found at last after days had passed
But nobody knew who he was.
He was buried that day in the field where he lay
At the foot of a soldier's cross.

Nobody to weep when the Endless Sleep
Drew a veil o'er his pain and strife.
May the soft, gentle rains o'er the hills and the plains
Be the tears for this soldier's life.

November 2016

Row upon Row

Row upon row of
white crosses and headstones,
marking Mankind's wars.
Symbols of human sacrifice.
Scars of Humanity's flaws.

December 2017

One of the hardest things for a commander to do is to write a letter of condolence to the bereaved; parents, a spouse, the family of a lost soldier.

I had occasion to write such a letter to an officer's wife, receiving a response from the widow in the form of a postcard. It depicted a deserted beach with the sun setting over the sea.

This poem is for the many, many mothers, sisters, wives, lovers, friends; all those who ever felt the pain of separation, and loss ... as a result of war.

Silently

Silently she walks along the shore,
On shifting sand she cannot feel,
With downcast eyes, for tears,
That see no more.
She stops.
But for the sea, she'd kneel.
She wanders on,
Enshrouded in her pain
For her lost warrior. Missing!
Wounded?
Slain?

1980

The Boy

He was only a boy
When he went to war,
Called to fight the Nation's foes.
He showed no fear,
But had a knot in his gut
That only a soldier knows.

Hunger and thirst
Were everyday wares
And soldiers his only kin.
His hands were hard
And his body was strong
'Tho his heart was quaking within.

It's the mothers who hear
Their sons at prayer
As the Shadow of Death draws nigh,
Who'd rid the Earth
Of this dreadful curse
That calls their boys to die

The boy returned
To his mother's embrace
And wept as she held him tight
But those wretched tears
Were not for his fears -
They were for boys who were lost in the fight.

1980

Operation Protea was one of the major military incursions into Angola by the SA Defence Force during the so-called Border War.

One evening, in the lager after a long and eventful day, I sat watching a spectacular sunset, undoubtedly occasioned by all the dust and smoke that yet remained airborne ... after the battle. In the twilight, surrounded by destruction and desolation, I spotted a small white flower.

The White Flower

War engulfs the land
In flaming rage,
And nature feels the scourge
Of some demented soul.
Creation's plan, writ large
Upon this ancient page,
Is scorched and scarred;
Remittance of life's demonic toll?

Marauding tracks crush
Unsuspecting life
As roaring, raiding monsters
Carve their trail
Across a landscape,
Innocent of strife.
This placid place, now witness
To destruction and travail.

Once-noble structures smashed.
Their smouldering beams
Leave wretched, ragged ruins;
Sad memories in their stead.
Yet in the wake of death
And shattered dreams
A small white flower, triumphant,
Lifts its head.

August 1981

How do you know that someone went to Grey College in South Africa? He'll tell you! Well, this is *my* chance. Yes, I was educated at Grey, the finest boys' school in the land. It was there that we were taught the value of team sports in the promotion of cohesion, *esprit de corps,* friendship and trust.

The hardship and danger, even the hunger and exhaustion, that was the shared experience of hundreds of thousands of young South African men during their National Service, also led to lifelong friendships and a strong feeling of solidarity between such men – from 1967 to 1993.

I completed one year at the Naval Gymnasium before joining the Permanent Force as a member of 1 Parachute Battalion in 1962 and maintained my cultural affiliation with my SA Army "mother unit" until retirement ... 36 years later.

The infantry, the gunners, the sappers, the troopers, the sailors and the pilots will all tell you the same thing; that *their* branch, corps, regiment or unit of the service was, and is, the bravest and the best. Good on them all!

In my book, South Africa's airborne forces, especially 1 Parachute Battalion in Bloemfontein, were the finest body of men that I ever had the privilege of serving with. They wear the maroon beret.

Mates in Maroon Berets

Oh, they know when you're not handling the pace
And they'll tell you that you're slacking, to your face.
But they'll always have your back,
They'll even help you lug your pack -
That's the norm, when paratroopers are your mates.

They'll drink with you until you hit the floor,
Then they're in your stick as you "Stand in the door!"
They'll support you in a fight
When no back-up is in sight;
And they'll fight all day – then still come back for more.

So, they brought you out when you were shot to hell,
When they could have left you there, where you fell.
That's the paratroopers' creed;
You can trust them in your need
And it *will* be so - until the last farewell.

Now, I've seen some hairy action in my day
And, by chance, have always come away
With no bullets through my hide,
But with gratitude and pride
For the brotherhood of men of the maroon beret.

1989

Our dad was a professional soldier. He was promoted to the rank of major during WW II and suffered the humiliation of having to revert to captain after the war. We never heard a word of complaint or bitterness from that proud and honourable man, who eventually retired, after 40 years of service, with the rank of major.

I think of him often. He introduced me to the writing of Rudyard Kipling, the "soldier's poet", and taught me to play Kim's Game. His favourite Kipling poem was Tommy; the one with the unforgettable lines:

For it's Tommy this, an' Tommy that, an' "Chuck him out, the brute!"
But it's "Saviour of 'is country" when the guns begin to shoot.

Tommy, written in 1890, could just as well have been written today. Soldiers don't ask for much ... just a little understanding and respect.

Salute the Soldier

Broken stuff and stupid kids,
We're told, is the soldier's lot,
As he's shunted all around the world
To the latest trouble-spot.

Their stuff got broken as they moved.
His kids went to many schools,
But they've travelled all around the globe
And they're anything but fools.

They've seen the African sunsets
And Paris in the spring,
Danced with Bushmen in Namibia,
Know the Swazis and their King.

He's carried his pack in the desert.
He's patrolled in the tropical rain
And when disaster struck, right here,
He was rushed back home again.

Soldiers take care of the hopeless
And the destitute, after the fray.
They'll stay to pick up the pieces
When others have all run away.

So, stand and salute the soldier,
His kids and their broken stuff
For, in spite of how badly we treat them ...
We can never thank them enough.

January 2020

This is not only in memory of my Dad, but also for our two highly successful, "stupid" kids, Ana Maria and Marius. I'm so proud of you both.

At Grey College, our English teacher was the inimitable Mr Jannie (Ploddy) Earp, whose eldest son Dennis, also an old-Grey, eventually went on to become the Chief of the South African Air Force.

"Privileged" as we were, Ploddy led our class of sport-mad adolescents through the gentler delights of Shakespearian sonnets ... in 1960.

My school assignment to compose a sonnet then was not a total waste of time; I managed to finally refine it (some 60 years later), fit, I sincerely hope, for publication.

Africa was aflame with decolonisation at the time, with British Prime Minister Harold Macmillan's infamous "winds of change", and I went on to become one of the Guardians.

Sonnet of the Guardians

Why is the human race so prone to strife?
Why can we not exist in harmony?
Instead, we ever reach for sword and knife;
When will we learn to let our quarrels be?
Creation's millstone has a human face;
Fanatics who are driven by their creed,
Who, flouting opposition and disgrace,
Would subjugate the world to fuel their greed.
But there are some who will not bend the knee,
Whose loyalty and courage you may trust;
Who cannot bear the thought of anarchy
And who will pay whatever price we must.
When threats emerge, we do not turn and flee.
The Guardians of this sacred land are we!

February 2015

Our God and soldier we alike adore,
When at the brink of ruin, not before;
After deliverance both alike requited,
Our God forgotten and our soldiers slighted.

Francis Quarles
(1592 – 1644)

Ah, how they prick their ears, those old war-horses, when they hear the bugle call.

I am now also one of those men with faded ribbons and tarnished medals on a baggy old regimental blazer, remembering old comrades and stunned by the rapid passage of time.

Fading Faces

Their numbers are slowly waning,
Old soldiers just fading away.
The pain that they hide,
Like their tears and their pride,
Is a price they're still willing to pay.

They went off to war without question
Seeking only the blessing of God.
Now, how proudly they stand,
As they did for their Land
When so many lost more than their blood.

We don't see them around very often,
Perhaps only on Armistice Day.
The "old and the bold",
In the wind and the cold -
For those who were lost in the fray.

Look kindly on these old heroes
For soon they will all disappear.
On each battered face
You'll find wisdom and grace
Of men who stood up to their fear.

Old faces, fast fading away.
Old faces, still showing no fear.
When the last one departs
Keep them still in your hearts
For without them ...
                you wouldn't be here.

11 November 2018

One of the immensely talented members of our writers' group, Ian Marshall, wrote a riveting short story about life on the Front Lines ... with a twist in the tale. I so admired his work, *Under Cover*, that I vowed to (one day) write a poem based on his story ... even though it would mean plagiarising the idea from his fertile imagination.

I've presented this poem to Ian for his approval and am publishing it, as a tribute to his skill as a storyteller, with his full and generous permission.

Ian's story, and this poem, point to the unintentional scarring that occurs when humanity makes war.

It's been several years, but ... better late than never.

On the Western Front

... inspired by a short story originally
written by Ian Marshall

The guns had ceased at midnight;
They'd stilled their cruel blast.
A shadow crept from tree to tree;
This night would be the last.
His limbs were aching from the cold.
His mission almost done,
He scanned for danger all around,
But sensed he was alone.

His coat was damp and muddy
From creeping through the woods
To avoid the many outposts
Where silent sentries stood.
He observed for just a moment
Then travelled on once more,
His camouflage concealing him ...
Like so many times before.

Then, from the blackness overhead,
The roar of engines came;
One hundred laden bombers
Out to spread their fire and flame.
The thunder of their passage
Would obscure his stealthy stride
As he hastened on to reach his goal -
His warm, protected hide.

He heard the quiet footsteps
As soldiers passed - like death.
His ingrained caution, hard acquired,
Forced him to hold his breath.
The threat averted; thankfully,
He tiptoed out of sight
And silently he slipped into
His haven for the night.

As calm descended in the woods
And the sounds of warfare waned,
He drifted off to some far place
Where peace and comfort reigned.
The darkness lifted as the clouds
Allowed the moonlight through.
He stirred but once, then slept again
... as hibernating hedgehogs do.

August 2020

A World Without War

I was born into a wondrous world,
'Though poverty was rife;
A world soon after two World Wars
That scarred 'most every life.
And even though the misery
Of war was fading fast,
The whole war-weary world still knew
That Peace would never last.

Before the dark clouds mustered
And the sun was in the sky,
The people snatched at simple joys
Before they passed them by.
The world was filled with promise;
Imagination led the way.
And there were children everywhere,
Who'd sing and dance and play.

But the human lust for power
Soon raised its hoary head
And children with no memories
Then ruled the world instead.
With no memory of suffering,
With greed their major vice,
They trod on basic human rights,
Not even thinking twice.

Two brooding powers, East and West,
Grew bold and preyed upon
Their unsuspecting victims
As the "little wars" raged on.
They called the conflict "cold war",
But the outcomes were the same;
Poor countries all around the world
Again, engulfed in flame.

Soon Africa, the Middle East,
The Far East, Europe too
Were sliding down that sordid slope
As discontentment grew.
But human spirit won the day
As people rose in rage,
Demanding opportunity
And a simple, living wage.

Still, Greed remains the driving force
And Dominance the game.
We see new prophets rise each day
In search of power ... and fame.
While millions feed on fruits of peace
More millions starve to death,
Yet, aspiring tyrants around the world
Cry War! with every breath.

The War on Thought, the War on Words,
The War of Who is Right;
The world is filled with "victims"
Where everyone must fight
For Justice and Equality,
For Gender Rights, and more ...
I wonder if we'll ever live
In a new world, without war.

I've lived a long, eventful life,
I've known both War and Peace.
I've seen it all and hope that I
Will see this madness cease.
If only "they" would listen
To those who've gone before:
The single cause for which to die
Is a World that's free ... of War.

May 2020

There is an expression that I heard very recently. I believe it may be ascribed to Robert J. O'Neill, the US Navy SEAL team member who reportedly shot and killed Osama bin Laden on 1 May 2011.

"Some men are morally opposed to violence. They are protected by men who are not."

There is, however, always a price to pay. I wrote about this in 2012, in the following poem.

The Sins of Warriors

For every lapse there surely is a cure -
Or must one carry guilt into the grave?
Should one attempt to live a life so pure
That mortal sins are never to be made?
We're taught that every sinner may be saved
No matter that his earthly life be scarred
By deeds, so heinous and so grave,
That, to him, the Gates of Heav'n be barred.
But he repents, the road to Hell assured!
Is this the path that every man must seek?
If this be so, what purgatory endured
By courageous men - defenders of the weak.
Admit to Heaven all warriors by their birth,
For they shall know a living Hell on Earth.

May 2012

Everything has a beginning and an end; a day, a season, a performance, a disturbance, a war ... a life. It is common practice for this and similar "truths" to be changed, re-worded and distorted by clever wordsmiths. That, however, does not detract from the essential veracity of the message.

The civil unrest that flares up every so often is used by militants across the world for specific, short-term political advantage – always with greed at the core. Planning is often "on the fly" as the situation develops. There is no concern for consequence, intended or not – and the resulting mess is left to the local authority of the day to clear up.

The following is an attempt to articulate, through poetry, my thoughts on the violent unrest in the world today.

Winter's Voices

There are voices on the wind,
As it swishes through the leaves,
That will alter with the coming of the cold.
For in winter, you will find,
As gusts clatter round the eaves,
That those docile voices suddenly grow bold.

"Close the windows! Shut the doors!"
The voices caution in the dark,
As the water in the trough begins to freeze.
Then a blinding blizzard roars
Across a landscape, grim and stark,
And driven snow rips foliage from the trees.

Stripping shingles, out of spite,
And flinging them about,
The wind rejoices with its wintry wail.
Shrieks of triumph shred the night,
Like wild laughter ringing out,
As windows rattle in the howling gale.

As the timid morning light
Steals across the frozen plains
There is stillness as the winter's voices rest.
But their moaning through the night
Will surely rise again
As the feeble-hearted sun sets in the West.

Yes, calm will reign once more
As the sun regains its power;
When the gentle voices of the Spring return.
Then the fright that went before,
At that darkest midnight hour,
Will fade before the peace
... for which we yearn.

August 2020

My son-in-law, Christo Rabie, is not only an excellent and dedicated doctor, he is also an avid gardener ... and it shows, in so many ways. This poem is for him.

A Strip of Prairie

A strip of barren prairie
is a garden,
and all *this* garden
ever needs to grow
is sufficient moisture, then,
like a pretty prairie tartan
it will banish winter's snow,
to let the prairie flowers grow
and to welcome in
the tiny prairie wren.

When you've seen
the prairie blooming
on a windless, sunny day,
the beauty of it
takes one's breath away.
Prairie crocus, Indian paintbrush,
Prickly rose, red Columbine;
the list of names alone
is a poem, all its own.

Surround your home
with growing prairie;
harvest joy, from spring to fall
For the prairie isn't barren, after all.

Fall, 2020

Many children in Alberta go back to school today, including our grandson. And so, repeating a process that began with the advent of modern humans, the seeds of knowledge will again be planted in the fertile garden of the future.

The pandemic continues to spread, but the Provincial health systems appears to be coping. The social turmoil, however, remains.

Violent mobs persist in rampaging through US cities, demanding "recognition", "freedom" and "justice". Why such trends in the USA should be imitated elsewhere in the world, is beyond me.

Parents and teachers alike, even we, the seniors of society, have a critical role to play in the education of our youth. What remains of our world, and the heritage we leave our children and their children, depends entirely on the seeds that are planted today.

Plant a Seed

Take a little time to plant a seed
and marvel as you watch the seedling grow.
Take only from the earth that which you need.

Spend some time to teach a child to read;
let your font of knowledge freely flow.
Take a little time to plant a seed.

Our world is presently consumed by greed.
What this will lead to ... we already know.
Take only from the earth that which you need.

Our children learn from us, we must concede;
We know that what we reap is what we sow.
Take a little time to plant a seed.

The attitudes to life that we should breed
should make us all our selfishness forego.
Take only from the earth that which you need.

We all prefer a flower to a weed,
Taking pleasure as we watch our garden grow.
Take a little time to plant a seed.
Take only from the earth that which you need.

1 September 2020

Note. Kudos to those of you who recognized this poem as a *villanelle.*

This is a tip o' the hat to those in my family and circle of friends who are contemplating that inevitable move to "God's waiting room".

"It is as natural to die as to be born".
Francis Bacon
1561 - 1626

Baby Grows

As every helpless baby knows,
along the journey, as it grows,
the day will come, for wrong or right,
when it will have to stand ... and fight.
However, babies have to grow –
there is so much they need to know –
from learning how to sit and crawl
and then stand up against a wall
to take those precious little strides –
and learning how to eat, besides.
The use of diapers, evermore,
will stop them sh***ing on the floor;
while giving them a walking frame,
will turn that chore into a game.
Those little teeth that gave them hell
will, in the future, serve them well.

But wait, the time has come and gone
and baby's years have moved along
to push the eighties - give or take -
along with hips and knees that ache.
So, now it's time to contemplate
what, in the future, lies in wait
for some old guy without his teeth –

who's wearing diapers underneath
his gown, with back side open wide
to show the ladies what's inside.
He's in a "home" with many more
infirm old-timers waiting for
the dinner-bell to ring, at last,
to call them all to break their fast.
His brittle pride, forgotten, brings
acceptance of unusual things;
a hearing-aid he cannot hide;
a walking frame that's now his "ride".
So, down the corridor he rolls
in comfy shoes with rubber soles.

Still a romantic – here's the proof;
his heartbeat has gone through the roof.
One wouldn't say he's in a rush
to see someone who makes him blush;
a lady friend, who's still a beaut ...
who also thinks that he is ... cute.
Thus, even when you're old and grey,
romance will somehow find a way.
So, here's a toast to bride and groom
together ... in God's waiting room.

September 2020

June 16 was "opening day" in Alberta, the day upon which fishermen were again permitted to visit the rivers, creeks and streams of our Province, fishing rod in hand. I spent the day fly-fishing on Racehorse Creek, a tributary of the Old Man River, in the foothills of the Rockies. Mid-afternoon it rained. I got soaked and there were puddles everywhere.

Later that evening I was scheduled to attend a meeting aimed at launching a project to involve seniors, the elderly of our Town, in creative writing. The aim was to teach, encourage and inspire seniors to engage in creative writing; memoirs, short stories, poetry. We, the trustees of the Library Board, were hoping to involve seniors more closely in community activities to alleviate, even avoid, their possible social isolation. Our chosen vehicle was creative writing.

Even as I was casting my flies at elusive trout and mountain whitefish, the meeting and its objectives were on my mind.

After the rain, I was inspired to write this short poem.

Puddles

After the rain
There are puddles everywhere.
Large or small,
Muddy or clear,
They are all filled with the same
Life-sustaining gift.

After the rain
All puddles reflect
The glory of the sky
And the stars
Or the sparkle
Of a sunny day.

After the rain
We must make time
To delight
In the magic
That the puddles reflect -
Before they disappear.

June 2015

Winter in Canada, in my experience, lasts for seven months, as my calendar revolves around the opening and closing of the official fishing season - 15 June to 31 October every year.

I now firmly believe that, *in summer you fish, in winter you wish.* So, clearly, much of my summer is spent out of doors ... angling.

Ode to Angling

Horse-racing is the fabled Sport of Kings.
What then could be the sport of common man?
Well, no other pastime such enjoyment brings,
To everyone, as only angling can.
On sunny days the flowers of the field
Will pale beside enticements of the stream,
Where gentle riffles sigh and kindly shield
The trophy trout, of which all anglers dream.
As morning sunlight creeps across the land,
Confining other mortals yet to bed,
The avid angler sallies forth, as planned,
To stealthily pursue his prey instead.
He worships in cathedrals roofed by sky;
And only those unschooled would question why.

January 2020

Fishermen ... and Idiots.

"There is a fine line between fishing and just standing on the shore like an idiot."

Steven Wright

I'm a fisherman, more particularly ... a fly-fisherman. There are those in my family (like my grand-daughter who, in her innocence, sent me the above quotation) who believe that, being a fisherman, I'm one sardine short of a full tin.

Having crossed the "fine line", the one that determines who is a fisherman and who is an idiot, I've become, I'm told, the idiot standing on the shore looking like an idiot. Let me say this about that:

Our idiotic world is full of idiots. Yet even an idiot will agree that acting like an idiot is probably not the most idiotic way of avoiding other idiots. And if standing on the shore like an idiot is indeed the best way to avoid such idiots, then even the village idiot will agree that it would be idiotic not to stand on the shore, acting like an idiot, in order to avoid idiots who, in order not to be seen as idiots, have no intention whatsoever of standing on the shore like idiots. Leading one to conclude that those standing on the shore like idiots may, in fact, merely be acting like idiots to avoid those that are so idiotic as not to realize that, in order to avoid the idiots, it is far from idiotic to, in fact, stand on the shore acting like an idiot. Which is exactly why I'm a fisherman, nay, a fly-fisherman ... to avoid the idiots, see?

So, who's the *real* idiot in this idiotic world full of idiots?

June 2018

The Gulls at the Lake

The gulls in our town, at Crystal Shores Lake,
O, such abuse these poor birds must take.
Driven by children from their own private beach
To a small wooden dock, temptingly out of reach;
Mewing and muttering in feeble frustration
At the human encroachment – without invitation.

As a fly-fisherman, not permitted on shore,
I've been here more than a few times before,
Angling from my tube or from the new dock,
And sharing the lake with the tenant fish-hawk;
Its cool, tranquil water, like a new sheet of glass,
Buoying countless blown seeds of tall prairie grass.

A solitary gull then takes off and glides -
On a thermal updraft from invisible tides?
Above me, looking down with a hard, beady eye -
Surely charged by the fretful gull-flock to spy,
It spots my strike-yarn from way overhead
Then swoops down to examine – a small piece of bread?

Not a whisper of breeze nor cloud in the sky
On a late summers' day ... that Bitcoins can't buy.
Just the bawling of babies and loud, happy calls
Of children, all splashing and playing with balls.
A warm summer's calm is descending and dulls
The sun-sated senses of humans – not gulls.

With nowhere to bathe and nowhere to play
I fear that the gulls must soon fly away.
Abruptly, on cue, the flock takes flight;
Up into the sun, 'till they seem out of sight.
Performing, out of pique, for the humans below
The gulls then provide a grand airborne show.

With shrill, joyful cries they swoop and they dive
Like tiny white gymnasts - for attention they strive.
They twist and they turn and tumble on high,
These avian dare-devils in a blue summer-sky.
The children look skyward at the shrieks of delight,
At the gulls, celebrating their God's-gift of flight.

We, earth-bound stumbletons[6], watch from the ground
At the feathered projectiles careering around.
No matter our fortunes, technology and more,
We're unable to lift up our carcass and soar
To the heights of the eagles, the gulls and the hawks
Looking down at the humans, like ants, on the docks.

The gloaming approaches, the humans retire
Dismissive of skills that they'll never acquire.
The gulls all descend from the heavens above
To settle once more on the beach that they love.
So, while humans have all that their bullion can buy,
Gulls are the richer - in their domain in the sky.

September 2020

---

[6] You won't find this word in a dictionary. It is gull-speak, for "aggravating humans".

The Secret Place

Known throughout the foothills, with his fly-rod he would roam;
He knew each stream and every living soul.
For years he kept returning, for to him it was like home,
Where the solitude, and nature, kept him whole.

This time was different though, for his pace was pained and slow;
It was his final visit to his secret place.
How he'd miss the Old Man River with its surge of melting snow
And the frost of freezing mist upon his face.

One day on Dutchman's Creek, while fishing all alone,
He'd found a hidden spot amongst the trees.
His camp for countless seasons, he considered it his own;
He'd not found another fisherman inclined to disagree.

The secret, how to find this place, was his to give. At last
He'd give his gift of knowledge, kept for years,
To someone who would cherish it, as he had in the past;
The secret to this wilderness, before it disappeared.

Someone else to see the sun rise over snowy mountain peaks,
To see the wild rose blossom in the field;
To catch a wily rainbow and release it in its creek;
To find his peace or have his latest disenchantment healed.

His grandson was the chosen one. He'd been with him before;
Once in the glory of a gentle, early spring.
They'd survived a frigid winter, took the summer to restore
And together shared the gratitude that only fall can bring.

They'd harvested the berries and watched the bear cubs play,
They'd stalked the spooky rainbows in the pools.
They'd talked around the campfire at the close of every day
And agreed between them that the wilderness was not for fools.

Rejection of his proffered gift had cut him to the bone;
There were other, better interests now, it seemed.
Thus, for the first time ever, he was sad to be alone
With his campfire, aching bones and shattered dreams.

He'd heard the stumbling in the dark and wondered who it was.
Perhaps someone who'd strayed and lost their way?
They'd be welcome at his fire, for a moment ... just to thaw ...
For in his present melancholy, he'd prefer they didn't stay.

Sudden silence of the insects was louder than a bell.
Then a youthful voice he knew rang through the trees,
"Hey, Grandpa, throw some firewood on that little fire!
Hell,
I cannot see to save my life and I'm just about to freeze."

25 May 2020

Random Haiku Poems

These poems came to me either as I was out fishing in the foothills or on a lake ... or upon arising in the wee hours of the morning.

Life is too complex.
How to make a better world?
Simplicity, friend.

Fewer friends are fine.
They should share your interests ...
But not your whisky.

A simple pleasure;
Teaching your wife to enjoy ...
Single malt whisky.

Uncomplicate life!
How best to take that first step?
Learning to fly-fish.

One hundred dollars
Needs not a snake-skin wallet.
Canvas is just fine.

Life is far too short
To have to drink bad whisky.
Let the barley grow!

Towards the end of January 2020, I was "fortunate" to undergo long-delayed surgery to my left leg ... before it was delayed once more due to the Covid calamity. Then, on 31 January, my much-loved mother-in-law passed away at the age of 94. May she have found the peace she so sought and deserved.

By early February, the novel coronavirus outbreak in China was becoming a major concern, with the World Health Organisation finally declaring the Covid-19 pandemic in early March. The early part of the year was a time of pain, anxiety and sorrow.

On 18 February, as if in sympathy with the dark days, our orchid at home bloomed, bringing hope and much-needed delight to heavy hearts. For almost six months those perfect flowers provided constant comfort and inspiration – just by being there in their simple, silent beauty.

Then, in the middle of July, the flowers fell quickly, one soon after the other ... as they do.

There is a beginning and an end to everything.

The Silent Orchid

I watched the orchid flowers fall.
For months they'd brought us peace.
As morning sunlight kissed them all
Our thoughts of darkness ceased.

Such simple plants, majestic
And so flawless in their form.
Humble, perhaps compassionate,
With neither barb nor thorn.

Bringing calm to anxious minds,
Comfort to those in pain.
Their silent presence, you will find,
Is balm to ease the strain.

Our silent orchid naked stood
As the deadly virus spread.
Its flowers did what flowers could –
Why not the virus spent instead?

I shudder as I contemplate
The sadness and the pain,
Then realize with vaulting heart ...
The orchid soon will bloom again.

July 2020

My Golden Years

Like Winter's frigid gift of snow
That soon becomes a chore,
The multi-coloured leaves of Fall
Mean work … and nothing more.

I contemplate, in foliage piles,
Just what one's life achieves.
After all the training, toil and time …
I'm now fit to rake the leaves.

Fall, 2020

That Season

See the leaves a' falling –
That season's come around.
The season with its calling
Of the pheasants on the ground.

It's time for heading home
To that warm and welcome place.
So, let others do the roaming ...
For it's time to calm the race.

Draw closer to the hearth
And sip of Nature's best,
For you have walked the path
And have fully earned your rest.

Now watch the leaves a-falling
Through the windows of your home,
And let others do the calling,
You no longer need to roam.

Drifting, falling with no sound,
More quickly by the day.
The leaves all tumble to the ground
Then simply ... fade away.

Fall 2015

Looking Back

When you look back upon your life and all that you have wrought,
On all the perils that you faced and battles that you fought,
Will you recall the sweetness of victories that were tasted?
Or grimace at the bitterness of chances that were wasted?

Did your efforts take you to the summit of perfection?
Or through years of turmoil in the valleys of deception?
Did you walk across the barren desert of frustration?
Until, with apprehension, you reached your destination?

You will have suffered pain and loss, as everyone must do,
But did you, while others failed, persist and battle through?
Did you love and were you loved? Were you callously rejected?
Did you steadfastly pursue the goals that you, alone, selected?

Then, looking back, what will you see – a straight and narrow trail?
Or a path meandering across both hill and dale?
A path that saw you taking all life's hardships in your stride?
Or were you timid and afraid, with caution as your guide?

These were the words my father spoke as I went off to war,
Words that have emboldened me to see the world ... and more.
And though I sought to circumvent avoidable calamity,
Just as he said, I often faced obstruction and adversity.

When I look back, what do I see? A journey long and winding,
Filled with opportunities ... for losing and for finding.
A life replete with laughter, with love and loss and pain,
And yet, despite my many scars, I'd gladly do it all again.

December 2018

The Story of my Life

I've kept a diary all my life;
Several, if truth be told.
What's happened to them?
I don't know.
They got lost as I got old.

This poem is for our married friends. When lust becomes comfortable, less frenetic and not so all-consuming, evolving into friendship, it becomes love ... the strong basis for a happy, long and gratifying marriage.

The stable, supportive and compassionate family unit is at the very core of a successful society. How devastating then, that the number of formal marriages around the world is falling, while the divorce rate is climbing. Research into the causes and effects is a sobering eye-opener.

Nevertheless, we admire and congratulate our many friends who have surpassed or stand on the threshold of their Golden Anniversaries. You all deserve our respect and every accolade for your fortitude, dedication and commitment to each other.

Corina and I will soon celebrate our own 50th, so she was ever on my mind as I composed this, my third attempt at a *villanelle*, for the anthology.

The Greatest Gift

The greatest gift I've ever had, is you,
Though it took time for me to understand.
Together we will see our journey through.

Looking back, I think I always knew,
Our life together took the path you'd planned.
The greatest gift I've ever had, is you.

We watched in wonder as our children grew;
Contented now, as on their own they stand.
Together we will see our journey through.

As twilight falls, I thank the stars anew
For the day that you gave me your hand.
The greatest gift I've ever had, is you.

The passing years like fleeting moments flew;
The hour-glass so swiftly dribbling sand.
Together we will see our journey through.

To many, many friends we've said adieu;
We're on our own now in this foreign land.
The greatest gift I've ever had, is you.
Together we will see our journey through.

September 2020

We retired in Canada, my wife and I, to be closer to our grandchildren and to be a part of their life. After all, grandchildren *are* God's gift for not having murdered your own children ... they say.

They were just nippers, ten and seven-years old respectively, when we arrived. Then, in the blink of an eye, the first was on her way to university in New York.

Change is constant, but it's also painful.

Fly

The time has come to spread your wings
To close your eyes ... and fly.
You'll never know what kismet means
Unless you go ... and try.

With all our love to speed you off
And prayers to guide your way.
Your dreams will take your life aloft ...
But wither if you stay.

You've waited all your life for this.
We've helped to make it so.
But now it's time to blow a kiss,
To spread your wings ... and go.

7 August 2019

Break a leg, my dearest Kiewiet.

Well, we started off with a poem about scars, so I guess we'd be okay with another, near the conclusion, right?

Our grandchildren are both active, athletic and competitive. Ever since I can remember, we've participated in robust outdoor activities with them, like skiing, for example. On Canada Day in 2019, however, I took a tumble, sustaining an injured Achilles tendon on their outdoor pickleball court at home. A year later I was still limping – a sobering reminder of the passage of time.

With parachuting in my blood, I've had some pretty spectacular "arrivals" in my time. An active sporting life has also contributed to an accumulation of bodily aches and pains, even scars – each with its own (sometimes comical, often hair-raising) story to tell.

Scars

Our scars we carry with us
Through happiness and strife.
They are the body's memories
Of youth, of war, of life.

A scar shaped like a sickle,
Which gave me quite a scare,
From falling on a river rock
That shouldn't have been there.

Another on my shoulder,
Collected in a fight.
Boys engaged in fisticuffs
Are not supposed to bite.

This scar here was not my fault,
Right here, upon my knee.
I blame it on a parachute
That dumped me in a tree.

But scars are not all visible;
Many hidden in the mind
Where no one else can see them -
Disguised and hard to find.

Our scars are really who we are,
They're what make us unique.
They don't make us peculiar ...
Or laughable or weak.

You can blame them on the whisky
Or the cognac or the rum,
But we'll bury you with all your scars
When all is said and done.

So, bear your scars with dignity
You've earned them, one and all.
And when, one day, you go your way
You'll leave the deepest scar of all.

July 2019

This is a fitting poem with which to complete the anthology. It is a simple acknowledgment that, without their womenfolk, soldiers are somehow not complete.

So, in closing this small collection of my thoughts and humble literary offerings, I salute my wife, and countless others like her, for standing beside her warrior, courageously … 'til his soldiering was done.

Canada, 2020

Ode to the Soldier's Wife

At that first glance he knew she was the one
And since they wed, she'd been there, by his side.
Courageous, 'til his soldiering was done,
She kept her word she'd given as a bride.
She recognized the dangers he would face
And understood the risks that he would take.
She knew he could be lost without a trace …
And every time he left, her heart would break.
She followed him wherever he would go,
And made their home a refuge from the strain.
She sacrificed all else to make it so
And never showed her heartache or her pain.
It's a toilsome path, to live the warrior's life.
More daunting still to be a soldier's wife.

11 November 2014

Postremum

There are scars
that have taught men a lesson;
One that every thinking man knows.
The most beautiful creatures
On earth, are women - when
Contented and in repose.

About the author/poet

Marius Oelschig is a retired soldier, a former South African paratrooper, instructor, staff-officer, military diplomat and commander, living in the small Town of Okotoks, Alberta ... in the shadow of the Canadian Rockies.

Having enjoyed an eventful, frenetic military career of some 37 years, he and his wife retired in Canada to be closer to children and their Canadian-born grandchildren. In retirement, he is finally able to pursue, focus on and enjoy his life-long passion for writing ... and fly-fishing.

He is the author of eight children's books, written for his grandchildren as they grew, an anthology of short stories, essays and verse, an anthology of poetry and the genealogy of the Oelschig family in South Africa.

He is also the winner of a number of literary prizes and awards which, in his own words, "... *while gratifying, also serve* to *fan the embers of the writer's passion.*"

Ever-ready to promote the love for and enjoyment of literature, he served as the Vice-Chair of the Town of Okotoks Library Board, spear-headed the involvement of the Town's seniors in annual creative writing contests and engaged in the instruction of Okotoks youth in creative writing.

As an avid member of the local writers' group, Write Away! , he is determined to continue writing well into the future. This will not be his last contribution to contemporary Canadian-South African literature.

By the same author

Wally

The story about what happened after Christmas.

Two Warriors

A young boy dealing with bullies at school.

Jessi

The everyday adventures of a nature-loving South African girl.

Scrap

The adventures of a remarkable South African dog.

Jak of the Bushveld

Growing up on a farm in the bushveld of South Africa.

Yeti and the Great TREK

The TREK (Trans Republic Expedition for Kids), to celebrate the Lion King's 40th birthday, is a rollicking reading-safari - from Cape Town to the Limpopo River.

The Wishing Stone

A children's historical novel about life in gold-rush South Africa.

Storm Clouds over Egoli

A children's historical novel about life in South Africa – before the Boer War. Sequel to The Wishing Stone.

At the Going Down of the Sun
An anthology of short stories, essays and verse

The Greatest Treasure
An anthology of poetry

Prussians in the Land of Proteas
The genealogy of the Oelschig family in South Africa

Look for the iconic toy soldier at the end and on the back cover of every book by Marius Oelschig

Manufactured by Amazon.ca
Bolton, ON

18444802R00079